MW01065749

THUMP

& other poems

poems by

Mark Madigan

Finishing Line Press
Georgetown, Kentucky

THUMP

& other poems

ACKNOWLEDGMENTS

Grateful acknowledgement is made to the editors of the following magazines
where some of these poems previously appeared:

The American Scholar: "Sidney"

California Quarterly: "Faith"

The Louisville Review: "Christmas in Milan" and "The Girl in the Hall of
Mirrors"

Poetry: "Letter to Monet"

Tar River Poetry: "Doors of the KGB"

Publisher: Leah Maines
Editor: Christen Kincaid
Cover Art: Mark Madigan, Astronomical Clock, Prague 2014
Author Photo: Mark Madigan
Cover Design: Leah Huete

Printed in the USA on acid-free paper.
Order online: www.finishinglinepress.com
                   also available on amazon.com

Author inquiries and mail orders:
Finishing Line Press
P. O. Box 1626
Georgetown, Kentucky 40324
U. S. A.

Table of Contents

THUMP

Ibis Hotel, Prague

Whenever I sleep in a new hotel
somewhere between one thirty & three
I'm woken up
by a series of odd-sounding thumps in the wall.

I say "wall,"
but it could be the ceiling the sounds thumps through,
a pulse that comes running from anywhere at all.

A thump through a drain pipe six floors up,
or a two-ton truck barreling over
a speed bump meant to slow things down.

I like to think
it's a young couple in their mid-twenties
engaging in wildly athletic sex,
an adventurous couple
with two very strong & now bruised backs.

But it could be a young man
frantically searching for his lost wallet
as he keeps slamming dresser drawers.

Or some psychotic airport man
practicing the way he scuffs up bags
that he sends down the luggage ramp.

Yet, sometimes, it's a softer thump,
like a child's bare feet
thump, thump, thumping across a rug
before climbing up
& leaping from the edge of a large double bed
that still might send him
crashing through the ceiling.

In the end, I suppose, its best not to know . . .

Like the night in college I was woken up
by what I thought was a headboard thumping
in the dorm room above me.

The sound was distinct, yet oddly erratic.
Did-it, did-it, the sound seemed to speak
before going quiet.

Then, in a moment, it picked up again,
did-it, did-it, it seemed to repeat,
before changing rhythms, *I did, I did* . . .

It seemed like gloating, so I had to know:
who was it who lived in the room above?
I imagined both burly well-muscled men
as well as skinny, engineering geeks.

Upstairs, snooping, the next afternoon,
I uncovered a double-wide room—
a rec room with couches & a large TV—

& there in the spot just above my bed
a wobbly card table was still set up
covered with pristine sheets of paper

& the old Olivetti that kept me awake
thumping through the card table legs all night.

THE GIRL IN THE HALL OF MIRRORS

—for John and Terri

That cold spring,
I followed the red flame
of a tour guide's umbrella
along the stone walls
of French cathedrals,
the winding galleries
of world-class museums
& chateaus stocked
with dusty bottles
of high-priced wine
& antique furniture
you couldn't touch.

But what stands out
was the blustery day
I ventured inside
the Palace of Versailles
to find a young girl
bored with tagging
along with her parents
had wandered a few steps
away from the cluster
of adults shuffling
from one long gallery
into the next
to turn pirouettes
in the Hall of Mirrors.

She stood alone
beside a tall window
that looked out over
acre after acre
of highly manicured
gardens outside.

The girl was no more
than ten or eleven,
& it was the flash
of her yellow dress
that I saw first,
the edges fluttering
as she spun about,
such gentle reflections
caught like butterflies
in the kaleidoscope
of all that glass.

As joyful light
filled up the bowl
of her small face,
what I remember
was her inordinate
concentration,
how she gently
straightened her back,
steadied her wobbling
self on her toes,

then raised the trembling
arcs of her arms
to spin not once
but again & again
before her father
turned & abruptly
snapped his fingers
as he barked her name,
& all the soft light
that once beamed out
from Madeleine's face
withered as she slipped
away from the stage.

FAITH

Sometimes, I believe
as a mountaineer believes
hammering his way up
the ice-crusted face:
there is no cradle of faith,
only the familiar shape
a North Wall Hammer takes
in the hand, the chiseling
sound the crampons make
eating the indignant ice.

A Swiss woman told me once
she knew a man so harnessed
in faith, he'd climb, alone
the treacherous North Face
of the Matterhorn. At night
he'd sleep in an orange cocoon,
dangling from a single piton
& the small web
he'd laced with nylon.

As long as light would allow,
the woman kept watch
peering through a small
& tarnished scope
she kept at the edge
of her bedroom window.
One morning, just as the sun
rose like an angry face
she saw him fall, his limp body
dropping like a red-headed doll
into a toybox of ice.

Sometimes, now, I still wake
wondering if the man
were jostled awake
before he slapped

the mountain wall. I know,
if the story were mine
to arrange, I'd say
he rode the short trip down
like a tourist asleep
on a midnight train:
never waking until
he crossed the border.

DOORS OF THE KGB

National Museum of Lithuania

1.
The first door strikes you
as oddly placed,

a tragic mistake,
a prison cell door

hanging here
in the National Museum

its steel bars clamped
onto soft yellow walls

but once you notice
the door is braced

atop two bricks
you understand this

was done for some purpose
& it gives you relief,

a kind of permission
to imagine this door

bolted down
in some other place

as you think about who
might stand at its threshold.

2.
There are no steel bars
on the next cell door.

A large iron slab
hangs as dumb
as a dead man hangs,
a hulk of a thing,
the rust-brown color
of a railroad bridge.
A single slat
is cut near eye-level
through this door,
with just enough room
for a small tin plate
or a bowl to slip through.

3.
Off in a corner,
   the last cell door
      seems to hover in the air

until, coming close,
   you see how it hangs
      on vapor-thin wire.

It's easy to imagine
   circling around,
      looking one way

through the eyes of a guard
   then looking out
      like a man locked in.

And though you might smile
   to see a young child
      slip a hand through,

you know this isn't
   anyone's artwork
      forged out of iron

but a large open wound
   trying to heal
      as the world walks through.

ANUBIS

It was the oddest
of gifts Wade left,
a twenty inch bust
of the god Anubis,
made from a dark
hand-carved wood
with nearly two dozen
bright gold stripes
set in the pharaonic
headdress he wore.

In the years I knew him
Wade kept Anubis
perched on the edge
of the black baby grand
commanding one corner
of his large front room.
There, most evenings
Wade would regale us
with stories of his lovers
in Estoril,
the cocktails, the dancing
& the long slow walks
staggering home
as the sun crept up
along the Portuguese coast.

But the week he turned eighty,
Wade left for his eldest
sister's home,
a small quiet villa
nestled in the hills
just above Florence.

So the windswept day
Anubis arrived,
in a shipping crate packed

with Italian straw,
I didn't need to read
the short formal note
his sister had written.
I just left Anubis
standing at the edge
of the wrought iron table
a few feet inside
my entry way.

He's still there
staring intently
at my front door
& there, each evening,
I like to greet him
as I toss keys
or scoop another handful
of my loose change
into the elegant
tooled leather tray
bought one March
in the bustling streets
around Santa Croce.

Most days he wears
my father's fedora—
the front end tilted
across one eye—
except of course
in the warm summer months
when Anubis supports
the team Wade loved
by wearing a black
Baltimore Orioles
baseball cap.

THE HEDGES OF CATWORTH

—for Bob Lookabill

1.
I couldn't tell you
whether they were made
of hawthorn or holly—
or whose job it was
to have them trimmed—
only that year
as summer wore on
their sharp claws
grew longer & longer
threatening harm
to the cars nearby.

2.
The hedges stood more
than six feet tall
& hugged both sides
of the narrow road leading
away from the village.
They menaced the end
of my morning trek
past Hail Weston,
Great Staughton & Stonely
before turning north,
just past Kimbolton,
to climb the steep hill
leading to Catworth.

3.
A blind turn stood
where the main road curved
around to the hedges
& there every morning
I'd hold a breath
as my car inched
out past the white brick

house at the corner
to see what was coming.

Most days—nothing.

But a few cold mornings
when the road was glazed
with sheets of ice—
& a thick fog seemed
to hide the houses—
I'd be startled
by the headlights of some car
ripping through the dark.

4.
Some days, after lunch
at *The Racehorse* pub,
I'd be stopped
by a farm truck lumbering
up through the hedges
as the hay bales stacked
in bundles above it
swayed back & forth
threatening to topple.

Without a clear view
to back the car up,
I'd have to nestle
the edge of my car
into the hedge
to let the truck pass.

And gritting my teeth
as I inched in,
I could hear the hedges
scratching their claws
into my car's finish.

5.
One morning, as a weak
winter sun came up,
an old man taking
his dog for a walk
was killed when a sports car
careened through the hedges.

His body was tossed
as the car sped off
but his dog didn't stop
yapping until his
Master was found,
a lifeless crucifix
wedged in the hedge.

6.
Days later, the hedges
had been shaved back
as if some angry
machine were driven up
& its steel teeth
unleashed upon them.

But the hedges' shaving
was badly done,
with maybe a hundred
young green limbs
hanging like limp hands
severed at the wrist
yet still clinging
to strips of skin.

Perhaps it was shock,
but speeding away
from that cruel spot,
I swore I'd never

return to Catworth.

7.
Still, some nights,
dreams take us places
we don't want to go.

Those nights I walk
a small nosy dog
through streets in the dark

a dog who tugs me
deeper & deeper
into the fog

until I feel the arms
of an overgrown hedge
tighten around me.

Try as I might,
I can't break free,
& no one's around

to hear me scream
when a towering machine
shaped like a giant

praying mantis—
with hundreds of chiseling
scissoring hands—

starts to descend
like hungry locusts
onto the hedge.

CHRISTMAS IN MILAN

—for Sarah McGurk

A few yards beyond
  the gothic cathedral's
    big bronze doors,

where clumps of snow
  brushed from the shoulders
    of visitors' coats

glistened on the warm stone
  as sunlight jabbed
    long red daggers

through the stained glass,
  I shrugged off the cold
    & headed toward the last

few pews in back,
  where I hoped to rest,
    to put the rumps

of my shriveled feet up,
  & let my soaked
    leather shoes dry out.

But I was surprised,
  to find how much
    I loved this slippery

trudge before breakfast—
  an old enjoyment, quietly
    seeping its way back—

since, for the first time
  in twenty-five years,
    as snow settled down

in thick wet sheets,
  I felt free,
    no longer tethered

to all my fear
  since I could get here
    without having to drive.

SIDNEY

London, 1987

I remember his laughter,
  how he told me I wasted
    the best part of the day—

the first few hours
  after day breaks—
    so tonight, after writing,

though both eyes burned
  from too much caffeine
    & squinting in the glare

of a small dim light,
  I took his advice
    & walked the dark streets

of the old Roman city,
  watching as dawnlight
    cast its glow

over the slate roofs
  of a city asleep,
    not yet annoyed

by the frost-coated windows
  of each parked car
    or the slippery walkways

leading to the doors.
  And, slowly, as the sun
    began to shimmy up,

& the city turned again
  to its rhythms of hot tea,
    shaving & newspapers

folded on a sink's edge
    while the showers steamed,
    I stood, for a moment,

in St. James Park,
    to conjure some words
    frail as the spray

of my own warm breath,
    & offered the smallest
    but sincerest of thanks

for the frost warming up,
    for the glistening tears
    of near pure joy

that I found, this morning,
    winking in the curling
    eyelash of grass.

LETTER TO MONET

It wasn't until leaving
the Portrait Gallery & standing
in the clatter of tourists, pigeons
& double deck buses in Trafalgar
Square, that I took to walking
down to the Thames, to lose dark thoughts
among the web
of quick turning alleys, bookstalls
& pubs.
               There, motorboats tossed
among the sunset's glitter
rocking in the waves; the spires
of Big Ben & Parliament stood
breaking through the fog; & over to the east
one young painter nestled
the river's edge, tracing the skyline
& shimmering landscape.
                                    Perhaps
it was vanity,
but as fog wrapped around, riverbirds
cooed & steel buoys rocked
& sounded on the water,
I snuggled close to the steel railing
overlooking the Thames
& hoped beyond hope—
as I wrapped a thick scarf against
wind coming on—the painter might place,
with a small black smear
just above the railing, or shimmer
of light just where the stone quay
reached down to the brown
& erratic waves, my soul here forever,
one crooked niche in an intimate landscape.

GLIMPSES OF DICKENS

—for Sena Jeter Naslund

1.
Forgive my smirk.
But what you have heard
is hardly the truth.

While Dickens did,
on the 8th of June,
suffer a stroke

at his Gad's Hill home,
he didn't linger
& die on the 9th.

Dickens recovered.
But vain as he was
he didn't want anyone

to see how scrunched
his face had become,
a look reminiscent

of the dark, scarred soul
of the lecherous Quilp.
So with the help

of a few close friends
he faked his death
to lead an elaborate

underground life,
based on his well-known
love of disguise.

2.
They rented a series
of small furnished rooms—

each one far
from London's hubs—

where Dickens could recover
as he kept up.

Though he would hide
in dark backstreets,

Dickens always meant
to wander again
the streets he loved.

Though now he's older
& showing his age,

I've seen Dickens dart
behind the bookstalls
down by the river,

walking by the docks
where tour boats head
downriver to Greenwich,

or resting by himself
on a small park bench

along the eastern
edge of Russell Square.

3.
But Dickens doesn't want you
to know he's back.

Still, I've seen him
dressed as a porter
carrying cases
at King's Cross station.

He must have dozens
of actor's trunks,
each one stuffed
with scarves & hats—

a mishmash of different
shirts & pants,
thick false beards
& wispy mustaches.

I've seen him, evenings,
on Chancery Lane,
looking for the nook
where Krook's Rag & Bottle
shop once stood

& Miss Flite lived
upstairs with her gaggle
of small trapped birds.

I've seen him caught
in the bustling crowds
around Fleet Street
before storming off
at a sharp, clipped pace
down a back alley
headed for the Thames.

I've seen him slip
into the snug of a bankside pub
where he takes lunch
& keeps a small room

looking over the water.

4.
Wherever he goes,
Dickens always stops
to take a look back.

I've seen how tenderly
he touches the tip
of one white glove
to the red brick wall
where the Marshalsea stood

then how somberly
he trails away
only to slip
in through the doors
of St. George's Church

not to drop down
onto his bad knees
but to see from his vantage
point in the dark

who thinks he'll play
the hapless victim
in a cat & mouse game.

5.
It isn't my goal
to try to trap Dickens.

Sometimes, though,
it seems I can feel him

passing in a sudden
shudder of the wind,

or hiding behind
a hawthorn hedge

as I stop to watch
the slow cascade
of evening light,

the way ivy clings
to an old brick house,

or admire the turn
of an ironwork railing

a few doors down
from Dickens' elegant
Doughty Street house.

6.
One cold spring,
  I spotted Dickens
    looking afraid.

Trying to evade
  school kids clamoring
    outside the Natural

History Museum,
  Dickens zipped by
    tour buses lining

Cromwell Road
  when suddenly hailstones
    started to pelt down.

Luckily Dickens
  could duck down
    into the mouth

of an underground walkway
  leading inside
    South Kensington Station.

After brushing hailstones
  away from his coat
    he tossed a few coins

into the hat
  of a tall black busker
    wearing a faded

Army coat
  whose mournful saxophone
    echoed along

the green tiled walls.
  When a train pulled up
    students & tourists

swarmed to the doors
  & Dickens was caught
    in a great wave of people

jostling to board.
  And just in the moment
    Dickens stepped on,

the train car jolted
  & Dickens was left
    with his face pressed against

a dust-covered window
  as the train doors shut.
    He was still there,

struggling up
    when the train headed west
    on the Piccadilly line.

7.
London's a vast,
    nearly impossible

network of corners
    & small side streets.

Wherever you go,
    whatever slim bit

of the city you visit,
    if you wait long enough,

if you keep an eye
    on those sitting idly

in neighborhood parks,
    or those souls driven

to wander the ornate
    halls of museums—

if you come to London
    you'll see Dickens.

Mark **Madigan** grew up in the suburbs of Virginia, Kansas, and Colorado, one of five kids in a military family. He always enjoyed reading, writing, and travelling. After graduating from Mary Washington College with a degree in English, he worked for the federal government and frequently travelled overseas. The poems in this collection reflect some of those experiences, with some poems being set in London, Paris, Prague, and Milan.

A perpetual student, he holds graduate degrees from George Mason University, Georgetown University, and Spalding University. His poetry has appeared widely in magazines, including *The American Scholar, The California Quarterly, The Louisville Review, Poetry,* and *Tar River Poetry.* "Doors of the KGB," one of the poems in this collection, was nominated for a Pushcart Prize.